Creativity Garden

Karen Guthrie

BookLeaf Publishing

India | USA | UK

Presentation by *BookLeaf Publishing*

Web: www.bookleafpub.com

E-mail: info@bookleafpub.com

ISBN: 9789360948252

First edition 2024

This collection is dedicated to Mrs. Jan Deyton. Thank you for teaching me to love writing and to let my creativity bloom.

ACKNOWLEDGEMENT

Thank you to Mrs. Lisa Degraw for helping me edit my poems. This book would not be what it is without your help.

Thank you to Shelby Snider, Inae Baek, Emma Whal, and Dayanara Clemente for reading my poems and giving me feedback on them.

Thank you to Lydia Stover, Abby Jones, and Sydney Trogen for all your encouragement through this project.

PREFACE

I have always been known as a creative person. My friends and family know that I love writing and that poetry comes easily to me. My students know that I love to teach writing, and love to read what they create in poems and stories. Writing is my outlet, my expression, and my passion.

But it was just that - a hobby and a way to vent from time to time. I had a dream to be published, but it seemed impossible. Writing slowly turned into a party trick, and it took a backseat to "real life."

The idea behind this poetry collection came from the realization that life does not have to be something that tamps down our creativity. It should be something that flourishes in every life stage we go through. Sure, it may change form with each life stage, but we don't need to hide our creativity.

I hope that this inspires you to spread your creative wings and find new ways to find creative joy in your everyday life. Read these poems deeply, or just quickly glance at them.

Color in the illustrations in this book, or leave them as they are. Use these poems as a springboard to inspire your own works of creativity. Write the thing. Make the thing. Sing the thing. Whatever it is, enjoy it and don't hide that light.

Creativity

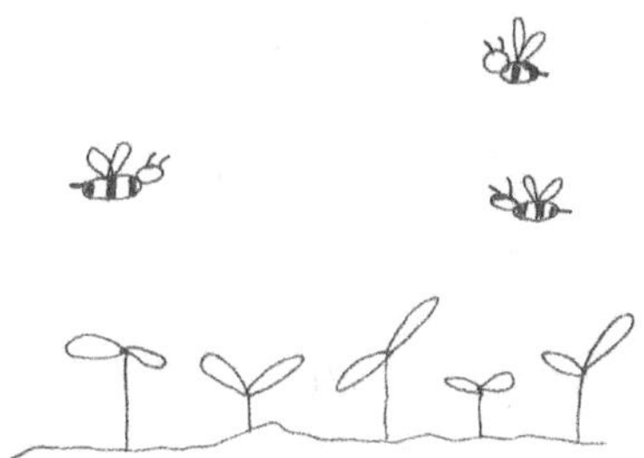

Who gives the seed?
The most fragile of things,
Delivered by His breath,
Nestled in the thoughts of the maker.

Who waters the sprout?
The tender, tiny plant,
Watered by His rainclouds,
Growing stronger with time and practice.

Who tends the soil?
The inspiration bed,
Tended by His prowess,
The maker's craft reflects the Master.

Origin

Blown in on a dream,
Fragile as the silk of a spider,
Unique beginning
Ferrying hopes of new adventure.

Precious, tended seed,
Ushering in vivid potential.
Sprouted, life-stretching,
Like sleepy bulbs in a cozy bed.

Emergence

Deep roots beg for rain;
Green leaves ache for sun;
And you crave the world,
My dear, Little One.

Texture entices;
Scents delight, it's true,
And my Little Sponge
Seeks to fill anew.

Eyes wide and alert;
Ears open to hear;
The flick of a tail,
The step of a deer.

And you, Little Seed,
Must take it all in.
Voraciously learn;
Growth sprouts will begin.

Budding

Little Giraffe
Is all neck and legs;
Gets what he wants
Whenever he begs.
"Do it myself!"
But can't use a cup.
Follows around
Like a lost little pup.

"No!" with a pout;
Arms crossed and a stomp;
Out to explore
To play and to romp.
Back home to Mom
For bath time and hugs,
Storytime, too,
With kisses and snugs.

Little Giraffe,
How much will you grow?
Wide world ahead
And so much to know.
Watching you learn
Your wobbly way.
What will you do
On your own today?

Growth

5

In this too tight tank,
Tirelessly treading familiar spaces,
Adventure sparks new;
Time to submerge in deeper ocean waves.

Trepidation creeps;
Fish, much bigger, cast overhead shadows;
Safety in the school;
Creative joy found in these new waters!

Innocence

Pirate ships and cowboys
Tag and hide and seek.
Swinging to the rooftops
Climb the mountain peak.
Telling scary stories
Jokes and secrets, too,
Shared imagination
So much fun with you!

Senses

Whirring of cicadas -
The sound of summer's call;
I am master-focused
For I can see it all.
I am no longer home;
My bed is far from me.
I hear the monkey cry;
The whisper of a bee.

The plants in my backyard
Are now Saharan grass;
Today I hunt the king
Who sleeps beyond the pass.
I brought along my gun
With bright orange on the cap.
I'll sneak up on my prey
Who snores, deep in his nap.

The countdown now begins
With "ready, steady, aim,"
A perfect shot well placed!
Imagine all my fame.
But quiet quickly breaks;
The Desert Queen appears.
My prey dashes away;

When her sharp voice he hears.

My desert is now gone.
I'm back home with a "poof."
I hear no pride lands sounds,
No roaring and no hoof.
In corner now I sit,
No gun or outside hat,
Because my game today
Was hunting down our cat.

Playmate

Favorite toy,
Treasured prize,
Comes to life before my eyes.

Playtime pal,
Adventure crew,
By my side the whole day through.

Snuggle friend,
Peaceful dreams,
Partner true in all my schemes.

Dreamer

The sweetness of dreams,
Like the first lick of a cone in summer,
Bathes the dreamer in imagination.

The most creative souls,
Sense it spilling from night into day,
Teasing that anything can happen.

Wonder

Who paints the flowers,
And pulls them to grow?
Why isn't starlight
Bright white like the snow?
Why can't the trees be
Red, black, blue, or pink?
Why doesn't water
Flow up from the sink?

If I made the world;
I'd make the sun red.
Flowers would grow from
A dark chocolate bed.
Clouds would rain candy,
And we would stay dry.
I'd make the world
With a purple-ish sky.

I have been learning,
With each passing day,
That all things were made
In a certain way.
Though there might be things
That I'd like to shift,
God gave us the world
As His special gift.

Pondering

Creativity is the water of joy.
We hoard sources to satiate,
Filling leaky buckets only to need them again.

A child's mind holds the deepest well.
Given, with no intent of hoarding
A treasure trove to use.

Somewhere, someone pokes a hole -
Another disappointing leak
Turns the bucket to swiss cheese.

If only we could trade with a child;
But our rarest commodity
Is held in a bucket with holes.

Sprouting

My Little One
Is little no more;
Combing life's sands
To see what's in store.

Newfound delights
Bring joy to your day,
Create and dream;
Remember to play.

Soon you notice
That others now care.
Don't dim your light.
Continue to share.

Not all will chase
The same dreams as you;
But one day you'll find
Friends that stay true.

Acclimate

Don't try to buck;
Just go with the flow.
Don't be too weird;
No star in this show.
Keep all your dreams
Down deep to yourself,
Toss them away,
Stashed high on a shelf.
Stand out too much,
You'll be knocked down flat.
Better to blend;
The world's just like that.

Glimpses

Passing days like sand in a glass,
Passing grades to finish a class,
Passing trends to follow the mass,
Passing notes, some filled with sass,
Passing years while dreams we surpass,
Passing time can't be stopped, alack and alas.

Blossoming

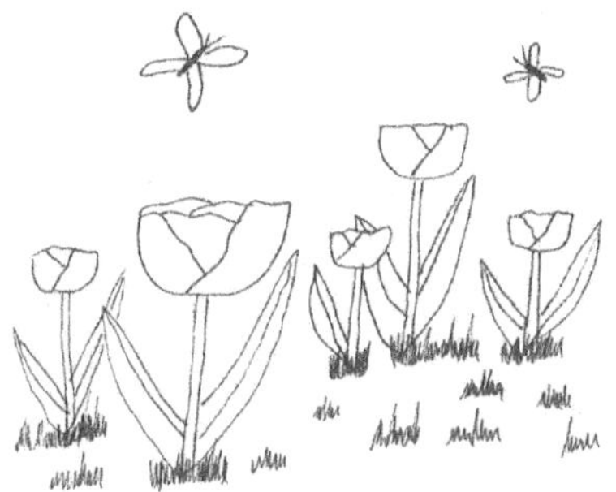

Shiny planner, day mapped out.
Clock is set, without a doubt.
Ready for a brand new day,
Doing things the grown-up way.

Breakfast first, then lunch is packed,
Brushing teeth, and homework stacked;
Have a checklist, that's the play.
Doing things the grown-up way.

Classes, sports, and projects due;
Squeeze in time for friendships, too.
Work a job to get your pay.
Doing things the grown-up way.

Choices

New page,
Crisp and unsoiled,
Ready for its marks.

Bittersweet -
Like the favorite toy
Now sprinkled in dust.

Two paths,
Creative and bold,
Steady and sure.

One choice,
With the deepest breath
He takes the latter.

Epiphany

The crash of the waves,
The thrum of the wing,
Each nature-filled thing.
The bow after rain,
The sigh after yawn -
All of these things as constant as dawn.

But…

The punch in at nine,
The rush through the day,
Bringing stress this way.
The traffic-filled drive,
The clock out at three -
These are the things that don't have to be.

Reminisce

Days blur
Like the view from ice-coated windows.
The light,
Now filtered in shades of blue and gray.
Mundanity
Seeps into bones like a rainy cold.
Forked road,
Like picking between cake and ice cream.
The path,
At the time, split between good and best.
The choice
Fading like a retreating sparrow.

Come back.

Recall

I've forgotten you.
The rush of excitement on Christmas,
The joy of a birthday candle's light,
The kiss from a wiggly puppy,
The squelch of a newly-made mud pie.

I've forgotten you.
The smell of the dirt after the rain,
The turn of the first page in a book,
The first successful bike ride downhill,
The wonder of camping under the stars.

I've forgotten you.
The one that believed that he could fly,
The one that drew the trees in purple,
The one that wished every night in bed,
The one that wanted to touch the moon.

I have forgotten the smallest me.

Equilibrium

While slogging through the daily haze,
A welcome sight did catch my gaze.
The tiny thing that I thought lost,
A rarest gem worth highest cost.

It can't be held as bill or coin;
It's not a thing you can purloin;
But I had buried down inside,
So sure creative thoughts had died.

But now I think I understand
This rare commodity so grand,
I found the path where once I stood,
The choice, I thought, the best and good.

Returning here it's now I see
That both the paths are one to me.
Creative joy, and steady true
Can both be walked as something new.

Return

In the stillness of the dawn,
I rise to start the day.
The birds are not yet singing,
Nor children out to play.

But here inside the quiet,
With coffee cup in hand,
I watch the gray horizon,
And see the light expand.

Then soon I hear the footsteps,
And see the smiling face,
I rush with arms extended,
And welcome the embrace.

This long-forgotten traveler,
This one I'd locked inside;
My inner child beaming,
Is now my joy and pride.

Generations

The lessons I've learned while tilling the
ground,
Each callous and bruise are treasures I've found.
For me to hide them from the light of day,
Would be an offense to others' pathway.

It's my job to teach the ones who follow,
When they carve out their own little hollow.
My own little one, and those down the road,
Can hear what I've learned and lighten their
load.

I'll point out the stones and hard-to-dig spots,
Encourage attempts by the tiniest tots.
We'll make things together, one day I'll see,
Lushest gardens of creativity.

Propagation

My Little Joy,
With smile so bright,
Please don't ever
Let go of that light.
Long time ago,
'Twas I just like you,
Stitched on a wish
To each star within view.

My Little Joy,
Though now you are small,
Some day ahead,
You'll climb any wall,
Dream any dream,
Make many things.
Just take the leap,
And spread out your wings.

My Little Joy,
Oh, don't be like me.
Dream and create,
And set your soul free!
Don't lock away
The treasure you bear.
As long as you live
Create with great care.

Reseed

As seasons change, the plants reseed;
The garden springs anew.
My thumb has never been too green,
I did my best for you.

I didn't have to move my roots
So sunshine you could take.
We expanded out our garden,
A place to grow and make.

Now side by side we learn and grow,
Creative thoughts we share,
We share our seeds with others too
So they can craft with care.

Climbing

Little Joy's first stride,
The toddling waltz,
Hands clapping with pride,
And learning through faults.

Laugh to enrapture,
Grin in a locket,
Wish I could capture
Time in my pocket.

But growth I won't stop,
Little Joy now shines,
New talents will pop
Like flowers on vines.

Exponential

Treasured plant, tended with care,
Watching you thrive as sunlight we share,
With time and love, plenty of room,
You brightly burst with colors in bloom.

Time kept moving far too fast,
But these memories are made to last.
Create, and make, and shine on your own,
Casting out joy with seeds you have sown.

Reflections

The flower I picked,
Fragile and fair,
Perfectly mirrored
Little Joy's hair,
Though long we had trudged
Through muck and mud,
We stopped for a time
To pick a bud.
Quite worth the slogging,
And puddle jumps.
Quite worth the struggle,
The scrapes and bumps.
While we both rested,
From our long walk,
The wind stole my bud,
Like a keen hawk.

Oh, My Little Joy,
Just then I knew,
It soon will be time,
You will fly too.
Flowers and children,
Grow in the sun,
But their time with us,
May soon be done.

Stunted

I watched you tend so carefully,
I tried to copy you,
But every time I tilled my earth,
My feelings were so blue.
Your plot grew lush and elegant,
You shared your seeds with me,
I tried to force the plants to grow,
But it's not meant to be.

My Little Joy, please don't you fret,
Today we'll plant anew,
We'll find the seeds that fit just right,
The ones that grow for you.
Nobody's plot matures the same,
We all have different skills,
Continue to create your way,
You'll make something new that thrills.

Jumping

Snacking on bugs,
Croaking a song,
Happy small frog
All the day long.
One lilypad,
Skip to the next,
Changing your mind,
Others are vexed.

But you small frog,
Content with change,
Jumping around
Isn't so strange.
You try it all,
Skip and a hop,
Bouncing around
The fun doesn't stop.

Small little frog,
What will you try?
Dream every dream,
Catch every fly.
Try every plan,
Make all the things,
Jump to the next,
See what it brings.

Gardener

It's okay to not know
What to try,
What to craft,
What to share.

It's okay to not try
Multiple hobbies,
Multiple projects,
Multiple challenges.

It's okay to not craft
In bulk,
In batches,
In mass.

It's okay to not share
Your ideas,
Your patterns,
Your energy.

But…

You should share
Your joy,
Your passion,
Your creativity.

You should craft
For fun,
For growth,
For learning.

You should try
To create,
To enjoy,
To inspire.

You should know that you can just start.

Trying

I want to be a poet,
But I just can't; I know it.
The blank page doesn't flatter,
And all my thoughts will scatter,
Do my words even matter?
I want to be a poet,
But I'm too scared to show it.

I want to be a painter,
But if compared, I'm quainter.
If no one likes what's pasted,
My effort would be wasted,
My tears, they would be hasted.
I want to be a painter,
But I am growing fainter.

I want to try some stitching,
But now it seems I'm itching.
My threads are now all knotted,
A dropped stitch has been spotted,
Into the trash it's potted.
I want to try some stitching,
But this one craft I'm ditching.

You want to be creative?

Art is interpretative.
Lots of ways to use your whit,
Won't take long to find your fit,
Just keep creating and don't quit.
You want to be creative?
Your thoughts are innovative!

Letters

Always
Be
Creative.
Dream
Exceptionally.
Face
Ghastly
Horrors;
Intrepidation
Just
Keeps
Learning
More
Notable.
Openly
Ponder
Questions.
Reach,
Stretch
Towards
Undetermined,
Visualized
Wins.
eXpress
Your
Zeal.

Harvest

With years paving your path,
Before colors fade,
It's now time to gather,
The fruit you have made.

Take baskets to market,
And set up your stall,
Share the fruits of your labor
With old, young, and small.

As they come to enjoy
The things you sell there,
Pass on all the lessons,
You learned with great care.

Sculptures

The garden floor -
To some the mess on their boots,
To others a tool for change.

Unyielding block -
Adding patience and water,
Adding creative promise.

Slow-growing craft -
Learn practice and persistence,
Learn balance and betterment.

Now pliable -
Handcrafted garden growing,
Handcrafted love to be shared.

Composition

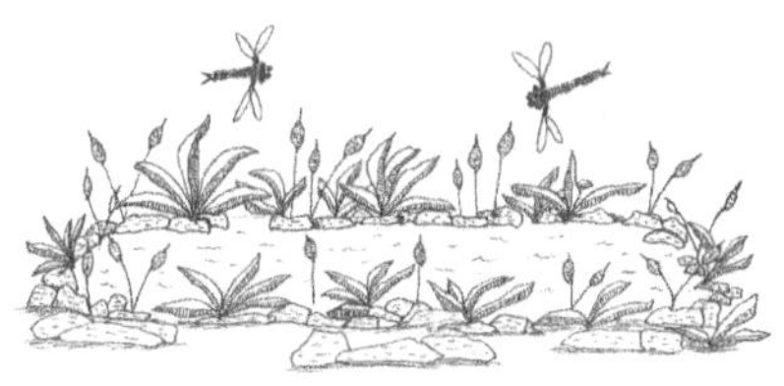

The birds take the melody,
While the worms take the bass.
The bugs like to harmonize,
Their wings hum out the pace.

Softest soot and pearl flowers,
Play formality's hue.
The dewdrops on the petals,
Make the sparkly venue.

This garden breathes in music,
Like dawn breathes in the day.
Creatives planting seeds here,
Float music bars our way.

Sketches

42

Textured, bound fibers,
An empty expanse of nothing,
Charcoal or pencil,
Scratching out a buried treasure.
I see vacancy.
You observe hidden potential.
Slowly appearing,
A gem of imagination,
Clearly visible,
Filling the void with brand-new life.

Stitches

43

Tiny X's marking the spot,
Like a map to the smallest pirate treasure,
They guide the watcher through the sea
Filled with holes, like traps laid out for hasty
thieves.
Counted stitches spreading their way
Across stretched fabric held taught by rings of
wood.
Picture formed of tiny X's,
The patience of the crafter on full display.

Photography

When the film becomes your paintbrush, and the light becomes your paint,
And your subject is so beautiful, it makes you want to faint,
Then it's time to set the tripod, and to focus up the lens,
And to gather up your subjects like you gather up the hens.
Shout out real loud "Ya'll smile now" and then holler out "Say cheese,"
Then forever seal that memory as pretty as you please.
Oh there's nothing quite so beautiful, it's hard to have restraint
When the film becomes your paintbrush, and the light becomes your paint.

Oh, it's never just as simple as a button-clicking press,
Yes, it takes a bit of mast'ry and a fair bit of finesse,
For you've got to know your settings, how to use them all just right,
And then how to set the camera up to work in any light.

But it's when you get it mastered and you have
your focused view,
That your pictures are an artform, you've
become an artist too.
Yes it takes a lot of practice and the patience of a
saint,
When the film becomes your paintbrush, and the
light becomes your paint.

Costume

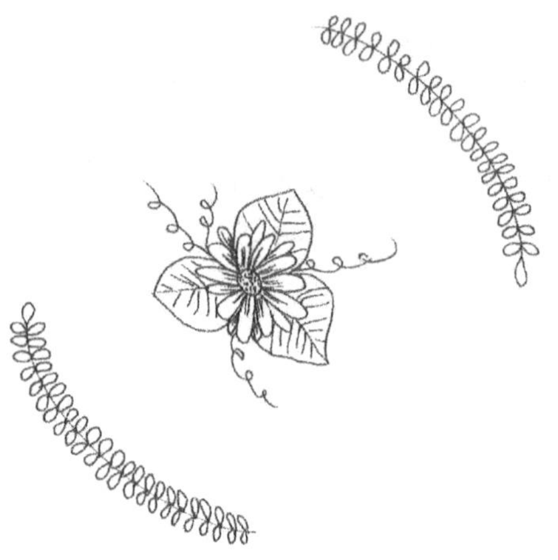

In and out,
Stitch by stitch,
Little at a time.
Clay and foam,
Glue and string,
Saving every dime.
Add a wig,
Makeup too,
Changing who you see.
Don a mask,
Play a role
That you wish to be.

Verse

So from where does it come,
This poetic hum-drum
That's stuck way down deep in my head?

Does it come from a dream,
Or from sparkly moon beam,
That splashes its light on my bed?

Does it come from a seed,
Of a feeling or need,
To be heard or to be understood?

Does it come from a care,
Or a burden to bear,
And venting would do the heart good?

Does it come from a song,
That moves life along,
An idea that's sparked by a friend?

Does it come from an ache,
When the long road we take
With a loved one comes to an end?

Does it come through the trees,

On a rustling breeze,
When a broken heart can't be whole?

I'm not sure when this came,
But I'm glad all the same,
And the words are a balm to my soul.

Quilting

Stuffed storage box,
Pieces and bits,
Saved scraps from memories past.
With tiny stabs of violence,
Soft threads joining
Old into new.

Wool

Knit and pearl,
Double and half,
Counting on each simple chain.

In and out,
Over and through,
Losing place will hurt your brain.

Hook and needle,
Fast and slow,
Tracking stitches is a drain.

Made and natural,
Cotton and wool,
Making something from each skein.

Woodwork

Master of chisel, and hammer, and nail,
Master of sanding and sawdust pail.
Crafter of table and toy alike,
Crafter for homemaker, crafter for tyke.
Maker of big things, maker of small,
Maker of wood for one and all.

Glass

52

On my own, I am rigid and cold,
Fragile to the bumps of life.
Sharp of tongue and touch to those around,
Useless without the Master.

In His hands, I am made anew,
Strengthened by His love and grace.
Sanded edges soothing to others,
Moldable within His hands.

In the flame, I am tested, made pure,
Master's hands sure and steady,
Melt and mix me with His colors bright,
Granting me His breath of life.

Through trial and testing with patience,
My roughness has been removed.
I am swirled with color and new life,
Now a masterpiece of glass.

Calligraphy

Careful strokes
Arching and diving on the page,
Like a dolphin in a show.
Linked markings
Inviting study through ages,
Giving patience new meaning.
Rules practiced,
Applied from traditions long past,
Passed down through generations.
Honored skill,
Yesteryear's creativity.

Writer

54

Read.
Read often,
Or enjoy the stories set in your mind.

Plan.
Plan details,
Or start with a blank page and nothing more.

Write.
Write hours,
Or only a few scratched-out moments.

Study.
Study others,
Or just make it up as you tell the tale.

Make.
Make readers,
Or make for an audience of just you.

Tasty

My workshop is my kitchen,
The stove top is my forge,
My craft is for the people,
Who surely like to gorge.

I craft the sweetest cupcakes,
And spicy dishes too,
I add in love for flavor,
Then serve it up to you.

This craft may not seem normal,
Or like some other kinds,
But I love making food art,
With tasty flavor finds.

Instruction

Everyone's garden is different,
You might not know what's ahead,
Petals of feathery brushes,
Or leaves of parchment and lead,
Or maybe you are the crafter,
Of pots to hold something new,
Whatever you choose to grow here,
Will help grow others' plants too.

Descendants

57

My Little Joy grew,
Had littles of her own.
Continued to spread
The lessons she had grown.

Those littles grew,
Each learned how to make.
In their own ways
Spreading joy in their wake.

Year after year,
Little come and grow old,
Passing lessons
New creatives will hold.

My garden grows,
Though my time is long past,
Lessons I sowed
Made creative thoughts last.

Pattern

58

Beware, beware the proverbial "They."
Question their expertise today.
Demanding you always do what they say,
Stating theirs is the only way.

Beware, beware the proverbial bunch.
Rip you apart with a quick crunch.
If you won't eat their advice with a munch,
They'll eat your effort up for lunch.

Beware, beware the proverbial clump.
Take some advice, the rest you dump.
For going your own way is sure to stump,
Your work, unique, will surely trump.

Alphabet

Any
Burning
Creator
Diligently
Explores.
Fervently
Giving
His
Inspiration
Justice,
Knowing
Life
Many
Not
Oblige.
Persistently
Questions
Rote
Skills.
Tests
Understanding.
Ventures
Wildly,
eXuding
Yearning
Zest.

Creator

It's been so long since the gardener came,
Those growing now don't remember his name,
But he's still here through the roots way down
deep,
In the birds that sing and worms that creep.

I study his lessons to do my best,
To spread my own joy and pass every test,
But how do I know if I've done it right?
To craft well all day and seek rest at night?

Then on the soft breeze a lesson is shared -
I learned from the Master who truly cared.
My crafting simply reflected the One
Who made the whole world, the planets, the sun.

There's no one right way to make something
here,
Create for His praise, for He holds you dear.
The One who created sky, land, and sea,
Has planted these talents deep within me.

Now it's your turn to reflect back to Him,
The talents He gave you deep down within.
Produce what you will, but make it your best.
Creating for Him is passing my test.

Solitary

If it's never seen,
It wasn't a waste.
It isn't distaste,
And your effort wasn't too green.

The days we create,
With fanfare or no,
Fulfill us just so,
And our joy we can reinstate.

Consider the blooms -
In desert alone,
Their colors propone,
And decorate sand-covered rooms.

But no one is there.
So why do they shine,
Their color divine
If no one is present to care?

They bloom for His bliss,
The One who did mold
Their beauty untold,
So their purpose was not amiss.

So go out and make,
With parchment and ink,
Or gold chains to link,
Your offering of praise he will take.

Praises

Praises! Sing praises!
To the One who Makes.
Tenderly heals us
Through all our heartbreaks.
Makes our way clearer
When we cannot see,
Gentle hands guide us
To where we should be.

Glory! All Glory!
To the Maker of All.
Made every creature,
Both giant and small.
Set each of the stars
And planets in space,
Made each mountain move
To sit in its place.

Honor! Give Honor!
To the Master of Skill,
Who crafted all life
To His perfect will.
Designed to reflect
Our Maker above,
Now we craft our way,
To mirror His love.

Blended

Your garden -
Flowers with silkiest petals and slender stems,
Beautifully lush,
Plants dripping from elegant, elevated pots.

My garden -
Thorns that give out warning and spikes that
intimidate,
Irregularly dry,
Vegetation in opposition to your own.

Our garden -
Cactus and flowers with complementary hues,
Scarcely artificial,
Greenery arrangements blended in harmony.

Varieties

I am a potter,
Molding words and notes into works of art.

I am a musician,
The whirring stone wheel is my metronome.

I am an artist,
My sentences paint worlds in your mind's eye.

I am a writer,
My brushes scratch stories into canvas.

I am a creator,
My garden spreads its seeds beyond my world.

Sunflower

You may have heard the meaning
Of the sunflower so bright.
The tallest, happy flower,
That prefers the day to night.
Tradition says its meaning
Is living numerous days,
But have you ever studied
This blossom's curious ways?
When sunlight is the brightest,
These flowers reciprocate,
Echoing the golden rays
They crave and anticipate.
When clouds filter out the sun,

As stormy cotton balls do,
These flowers find nearby friends
To distribute light into.
I wonder if that lesson,
That flowery secret stare,
Is that we live much longer,
When our light with friends we share.

Spreading

Sharing is scary.
Giving up that hidden piece,
Breath short, chest tightens.

Someone picks it up,
Cherishes that part of you,
Inspiration spreads.

But sometimes they don't.
Be patient, wait for the wind
To carry you home.

Display

Welcome to the grand art show!
I'm the curator here.
This collection is not new,
It's very old, My Dear.
We brought it up from storage
To let it see the light,
Usually these pieces show
In the loneliness of night.

Here you'll find a wide array
For both the young and old.
Our artist has some doozies
Of stories never told.
She masterfully pours them
In each new art piece here,
And carefully she stores them
For viewing times each year.

The first one hangs in honor,
The oldest one we have,
Created over decades
It oozes like a salve.
You notice it's not healing,
That's not the purpose here,
It's made from hurtful comments

Collected through the years.

Now this one is a treasure,
A contrast to be sure,
It shows the peace and treasure
Of friendships that endure.
Not all the art that's made here,
Comes from a painful burr,
But every brushstroke present,
Contains a piece of her.

Thank you for your time today,
I'll leave you to peruse.
Let the artwork speak to you,
Each joy spot and each bruise.
Our artist does have one wish,
Please keep this in your mind,
Words always stain like pigments,
Remember to be kind.

Blocked

I was going to write,
A poem to delight,
To show you my talent so smart.

My words are all muddled,
My brain quite befuddled,
I simply don't know where to start.

When I try to create,
Or perhaps imitate,
At times I'm trapped deep in the muck.

Creativity needs,
My persistence as seeds,
I'll write a way to get unstuck.

Inspiration

When inspiration up and leaves,
I go stepping out my door,
To make creative juices flow,
And ideas start to soar.

This morning the sky was painted
With a beautiful array,
The Great Master used his paintbrush
To make the most grand display.

He dipped his brush in fluffy clouds,
Dabbing each into their place,
He swirled in shades of darkest gray,
Letting raindrops fill some space.

He then broke up the dark gray spots
With some patches of bright blue,
Then brightened up the whole wide sky
With soft sunlight peeking through.

The mix of gray, and blue, and sun,
From only a Master's touch,
Sky turned canvas did inspire,
I'm ready to craft so much.

Gazebo

The painter seeds are planted,
And actor grasses too,
Musician bushes blossom,
With notes of every hue.
The potter wheels are turning,
In Watercolor Lake,
And baker topiaries,
Smell just like Grandma's cake.
The space that I have claimed here,
The perfect place to be,
The Writer's Nook Gazebo,
Full garden view for me.

Beauty

Like the moth at the porch light,
I am drawn to beauty,
Yet beauty alone cannot my soul alight.

'Tis the nectar of making,
Mixed with practice and care,
That the thing, once made, brings healing to the
soul.

Rest

Put it aside.
When ideas start to wander,
And you can no longer ponder,
Then your time you shouldn't squander.
Put it aside.

Put it down.
When frustration starts to boil,
And your happiness might spoil,
Take some time away from toil.
Put it down.

Put it away.
It's okay to come back later,
When some rest you need to cater,
Inspiration comes back greater.
Put it away.

Dedication

Time is the gentle rainfall
That waters crafted roots.
With patient soil mixes
To feed the little shoots.
Rehearsal is the sunlight
That makes the leaves turn green.
Passion places mulch around
To beautify the scene.
Commitment stands there guarding
O'er tender works of skill,
Holding careful vigilance,
'Till growing's had its fill.
At first a tiny growth spurt,
But with persistence true,
The craft becomes a showpiece,
A masterwork to view.

Artistry

Who can observe the thinking
Inside the maker's head?
Or watch the dreams he's dreaming
While slumbering in bed?
It surely is not us,
This audience outside,
But when we stand there viewing,
His vision is applied.

Who can perceive our cravings
That dig an empty hole?
Or understand the noises
That burdens down our soul?
It surely is not he,
The crafter of the thing.
Yet there with composition,
Fulfillment he can bring.

Mirror

Made in your image,
Yet fragile and small,
You are Creator,
And Maker of All.
How then can I be
A mirror of You;
Finish the calling
You've asked me to do?

Talents You've given,
But all on my own,
I wander aimless,
Unfocused alone.
Please guide my footsteps;
Show me the way.
Use me to serve You;
Mold me like clay.

In Master's workshop,
I listen and learn,
Build up my talents,
And practice in turn.
Trusting His guidance,
My skills are refined,
Casting His image
That's now more defined.

Sharing

Over warmest cup of coffee in the local coffee
shop,
Domestic gossip grannies meet, their stories now
to swap.
Across the busy highway tucked inside a cozy
nook,
Is a writer doing research for her latest romance
book.
And somewhere in the city, in a room with walls
of white,
And a whiteboard filled with scribbles and a
deadline very tight,
Is a group of tired workers with a frazzled kind
of air,
But ideas are encouraged here, so everyone will
share.
Yes all over the city, and out in the country too,
There are people sharing concepts just to help
make something new.
And that's the secret really, yes all makers are
aware,
That inspiration blossoms when ideas we all
share.

Example

Then after six days,
Of creative blaze,
And taking in the whole span,
The Maker of All,
Of both great and small,
Halted His powerful plan.

He chose to find rest,
His creation was best,
Everything made there was good.
From work He'd been freed,
And though there was no need,
He rested, just as we should.

Now in this pattern still,
We reflect His great will,
When working, we give our all.
But when labor is done,
Our reward has been won.
We savor respite's sweet call.

Stars

Blanket of grass to rest on,
Sparkles on velvety sky,
Wondrous beauty of starlight,
No one could ever deny.

A day of work completed,
Now it's time for well-earned rest.
The night sky up above you;
Inspiration at its best.

All effort is expended,
Time for peace and dreams so sweet,
Tomorrow brings new making,
New ideas to complete.

For now sleep well, Dear Maker,
Delight in starlight above,
May inspiration guide you,
To share your talents with love.

Epilogue

I did not get my poems
From those who count each line.
Nor did I get my wordcraft
From those who almost rhyme.
I did not find my deepest joy
From sonnets or haiku.
I didn't come to love it
Because school taught me to.

The creative part of me
Comes from my God above,
So I write poems for others,
To tell them of His love.
I cannot simply tell you
Why I so love to rhyme,
But using it to praise Him,
Best uses up my time.